Johnny Appleseed

Johnny Appleseed

by Gwenyth Swain

illustrations by Janice Lee Porter

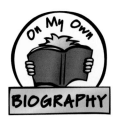

On My Own
BIOGRAPHY

M Millbrook Press/Minneapolis

Leominster, Massachusetts
September 26, 1774

It's a boy!
Someone must have told
Nate Chapman the news.
Nate and Elizabeth Chapman
had just had their second child.
They called the baby boy John.

6

John Chapman's childhood
didn't last long.
He grew up fast.
Before he was two years old,
his father had left to be a soldier.
Nate was fighting the British
in the Revolutionary War.

John's mother missed Nate.

Most women in the 1700s

could not read or write.

But Elizabeth could.

In June 1776,

she wrote Nate a long letter filled with love.

"Our children are both well," she told Nate.

Then she told him the bad news.

"I think I grow weaker," she wrote.

"I desire your prayers for me."

Mrs. Chapman was sick.

She would soon be having a new baby.

There was no money to buy a cow.

Warm, healthy milk might have made her

and the baby better.

But by July, she was dead.

The baby died soon after.

John and his sister, Elizabeth,

were almost all alone in the world.

Family and friends

most likely took them in while their

father fought in the war.

After the war ended,

Nate came back home.

John and Elizabeth may have wanted

to have their father to themselves.

But they didn't get their wish.

Nate Chapman soon remarried.

He and his children

and his new wife, Lucy,

moved to the town of Longmeadow.

In a few years,

their home was bursting with children.

John and Elizabeth had
ten half-brothers and half-sisters.
That many brothers and sisters
could make any house seem small.
John roamed outside
whenever he got a chance.
There were rivers to explore.
Where would they take him?

There were woods beyond town.
What better place to stretch his long legs?
John loved the peace and quiet
of rivers and woods.
When he was still a young man
he headed off into the frontier.
In the 1790s,
the frontier began in Pennsylvania.

Frontiersman

People who met John in Pennsylvania
remembered him.
He was young and strong and friendly.
He was a man who liked to roam.
One time, John got caught
in a snowstorm in the wilderness.
He had no shoes on.
It had been warm before the storm.
But John knew what to do.
He wrapped his feet in cloth.
He made snowshoes from tree branches.
And he walked out alive
from the worst storm
most people could remember.
Stories like that seemed to follow John
wherever he went.

Around 1797,
John went to Warren, Pennsylvania.
It was hardly even a town.
But people were heading there
by the wagonload.

They wanted to build cabins and farms.

John had other plans.

He figured others could clear the land
and farm it.

He was going to plant trees . . .

. . . apple trees.

Planting Seeds

Planting apple seeds was hard work.
John was always bending, digging, and
dropping another seed
into the dirt.
Planting apple seeds took time.
John checked on his young trees
a few times a year.
He built fences of brush.
That kept the deer from eating
all the leaves in spring.

Planting apple seeds was lonely.
John planted orchards
on land that nobody owned.
Blue jays chattered to him from the trees.
Deer left paths showing him the way
to clear, cool streams.

When John camped out at night,
he treated the mosquitoes
like long-lost friends.
He ate his dinners cold.
That way his campfire
wouldn't hurt a fly.

John didn't grow apple trees
to keep him company.
He didn't grow them
because it was fun.
He grew apple trees to sell
to new settlers.
Settlers were moving to
Pennsylvania because land was cheap.
But to keep the land,
they had to improve it
in two years.

Two years wasn't a long time
to carve a farm
out of the wilderness.
John's apple seeds were little trees
by the time most settlers arrived.
A settler who bought John's trees
to make a little orchard
improved his land.
And he hardly had
to lift a finger.

If you were a settler,

building a cabin or planting corn,

you'd be happy to buy

some of John's young apple trees.

In a few years,

apple tree seedlings

would be big enough to bear fruit.

Fruit was good food

for a hungry settler.

John stopped by new cabins.

Settlers were glad to welcome him.

They invited John in for supper.

They asked if he wanted
to stay the night.

And most asked if they could buy
apple trees.

Some settlers paid John in cash.

Others paid him in cornmeal
or clothes or conversation.

It was a good life for John.

A Good Friend

Soon the land was chock-full
of settlers.
The frontier was moving farther west.
So around 1801,
John grabbed his bags
of apple seeds.
He moved farther west, too.

John started new orchards

in Ohio, Michigan, and Indiana

before they were states.

There were only scattered towns.

There were almost no roads.

Everyone followed rivers and creeks.

Everyone walked on trails

the local Indians had made in the woods.

Everyone, including the Indians.

John was friendly
with Indians he met.
He was friendly
with white settlers, too.
In 1812,
he got stuck between friends.
The British were fighting
the Americans again.
They were at war on the frontier.
The Indians took sides
with the British.
Some Indians attacked white settlers
in their cabins in northern Ohio.
John Chapman said he'd go south
to warn other settlers.
Someone had to get help.

All day and all night,
John traveled.
He went alone through
the dark, dark woods.
John never stopped
except to warn settlers
at lonely cabins.
Finally he reached a town with soldiers.
The soldiers John talked to
rushed up north.
They killed all the Indians,
even ones who hadn't hurt settlers.
John nursed his sore feet
and shook his head.
Had he done the right thing
after all?

Spreading the News

At some point in John's life,
God spoke to him.
Maybe he was walking
on a trail in the woods
thinking about his dead friends.
Maybe he was reading the Bible
alone by the fire at night.

Or maybe he was planting apple seeds
in the wilderness.
Somewhere, somehow, John found God.
And once John found God,
he had to spread the news.
John traveled from town to town.
He still planted apple seeds.
But he also planted God's word.

John stopped whenever he found

a few cabins close together.

He stopped when he found

a good clearing in the woods.

Then he yelled as loud as he could.

He yelled that he had the

"news right fresh from heaven."

No one wrote down John's sermons.

But grown-ups liked what they heard.

Children liked John, too.

He always mixed tales of his travels

with what he read from the Bible.

Settlers on the frontier were hungry for

news and for company.

John's sermons filled them right up.

The Real Johnny Appleseed

John never married.
Maybe it was because
he was always on the move.
He never had sons or daughters
or grandchildren.
But he did have "children" of sorts.
All through Pennsylvania, Ohio,
Indiana, and Michigan,
he left apple trees behind him.

John Chapman died in 1845
in Fort Wayne, Indiana.
Later, the people of Fort Wayne
made a park at the place
where they *think* John was buried.
Like many things about John,
people aren't sure of the facts.
And when facts are scarce,
people often pass on stories—
stories that may or may not be true.

In one story,

someone called him Johnny Appleseed.

The name stuck.

Before you knew it,

people thought *Johnny*

had always been John's name.

In another story,

folks said John wore a tin pot for a hat.

They said he never wore shoes.

They claimed he had a coat

made from burlap sacks.

When John traveled around,

no one ever mentioned

him wearing a pot on his head.

Or wearing burlap sacks.

If they didn't mention these things,

it's likely John dressed

the same way settlers did.

A man named Haley wrote a story about
John for *Harper's Magazine* in 1871.
Haley repeated stories
people had been telling
about John Chapman for years.
Some were true.
Some were not.
Historians are still trying
to sort out one from the other.

Who was the *real* Johnny Appleseed?

He lived and died a long time ago.

We may never know all the facts.

But some folks claim

you can still find apple trees

that he planted.

Next time you eat an apple,
remember a man named John.
He lived on the rough frontier.
He brought people
the "news right fresh from heaven."
And he planted hope,
along with apple seeds.

Johnny Appleseed as he appeared in *Harper's Magazine* in 1871.

Important Dates

1774—John Chapman is born in Leominster, MA, on September 26 to Nathaniel and Elizabeth Chapman.

1776—John's mother dies on July 18. John is almost two years old, and his older sister, Elizabeth, is nearly six. Their little brother, Nate, dies soon after.

1779—John's father marries 18-year-old Lucy Cooley.

1797-98—John, at age 23, travels along the Allegheny River in western Pennsylvania, an area just opened up for European settlement. John is believed to have planted apple seeds on Brokenstraw Creek, near Warren, PA.

1801-04—John plants apple seeds near Owl Creek (now Center Run), OH.

1809—John, at age 35, buys the first land he ever owned—town lots in Mount Vernon, OH.

1812—John travels from Mansfield to Mount Vernon to warn settlers of a possible Indian attack.

1817—John begins work as a missionary for the Church of the New Jerusalem, preaching the doctrines of Emanuel Swedenborg.

1845—John is thought to have died on March 18 of "the winter plague" in Fort Wayne, IN.

Bibliography

Fincken, Hank. "Johnny Appleseed: Cutting to the Core." *Traces of Indiana and Midwestern History*, Winter 1995, 38–43.

Haley, W. D. "Johnny Appleseed: A Pioneer Hero." *Harper's New Monthly Magazine*, November 1871, 830–36.

Harris, Robert C. *Johnny Appleseed Source Book*. Fort Wayne, IN: Public Library of Fort Wayne and Allen County, 1956.

Pershing, Henry A. *Johnny Appleseed and His Time*. Strasburg, VA: Shenandoah Publishing House, 1930.

Price, Robert. *Johnny Appleseed: Man and Myth*. Bloomington, IN: Indiana University Press, 1954.